KINGS & QUEENS of England

Illustrated largely by Donna Neary
Text from the best sources by David Brownell and Harry Knill

On the front cover is Richard II, 1386; National Portrait Gallery, London

A god is not so glorious as a king.
I think the pleasure they enjoy in heaven
Cannot compare with kingly joys in earth.
To wear a crown enchased with pearl and gold,
Whose virtues carry with it life and death;
To ask and have, command and be obeyed;
When looks breed love, with looks to gain the prize—
Such power attractive shines in princes' eyes!
—Christopher Marlowe, *Tambburlaine the Great*

Oh, 'tis but a glorious thing, I ween,
To be a regular Royal Queen!
No half-and-half affair, I mean,
No half-and-half affair,
But a right-down regular Royal Queen!
—W. S. Gilbert, *The Gondoliers*

I think the king is but a man, as I am: the violet smells to him as it doth to me; the element shows to him as it doth to me; all his senses have but human conditions: his ceremonies laid by, in his nakedness he appears but a man. . .
—Shakespeare, *Henry V*, the king before the battle

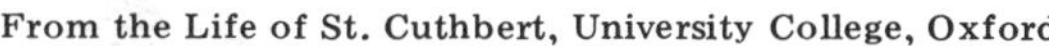

From the Life of St. Cuthbert, University College, Oxford

From the Charter of New Minster, Westminster, British Museum

Offa of Mercia
757 - 796

Beornwulf of Mercia
823 - 825

Athelstan of East Anglia
c. 794 - 855

Ragnald of York
919? - 921?

Ethelred Unraed
979 - 1016

Ethelbert of the East Angles
c. 794

Ludecan of Mercia
825 - 827

Ethelred I of Northumbria
774 - 796

Athelstan of the West Saxons
925 - 939

Edmund Ironside
1016

Coenwulf of Mercia
796? - 821

Baldred of Kent
c. 825

Alfred of the West Saxons
871 - 899

Edred of the West Saxons
946 - 955

Harold Harefoot
1035 - 1040

Cuthred of Kent
798 - 807

Eanred of Northumbria
807 - 840

Ceolwulf II of Mercia
874? - 886?

Edwig
955 - 959

Harthacnut
1040 - 1042

Egbert of the West Saxons
802 - 839

Beorhtwulf of Mercia
840 - 852

Edward the Elder of the West Saxons
899 - 925

Edgar
959 - 975

Edward the Confess
1042 - 1066

Ceolwulf I of Mercia
821 - 823

Burgred of Mercia
852 - 874

Halfdan of York
902? - 909

Edward the Martyr
975? - 979

Harold Godwinson
1066

". . . before him there was never so great a king of England. He was lord of the whole of Denmark, England, and Norway; as also of Scotland.

. . . when at the summit of his power, he ordered a seat to be placed for him on the sea-shore when the tide was coming in; thus seated, he shouted to the flowing sea, 'Thou, too, art subject to my command, as the land on which I am seated is mine; and no one has ever resisted my commands with impunity. I command you, then, not to flow over my land, nor presume to wet the feet and robe of your lord.' The tide, however, continuing to rise as usual, dashed over his feet and legs without respect to his royal person. Then the king leaped backwards, saying:

'Let all men known how empty and worthless is the power of kings, for there is none worthy of the name but He whom heaven, earth, and sea obey by eternal laws.'"

—Henry Of Huntingdon's *Chronicle*

CANUTE
1016 - 1035

Merrily sang the monks in Ely
When Cnut, King, rowed thereby;
'Row, my knights, near the land,
And hear we these monks' song.'

—a fragment of Anglo-Saxon poetry

Cnut & Aelfgyfu, from the New Minster Register, Winchester, 1020-30; British Museum

White beard and moustache; gold crown, sceptre, orb and brooch; gold tunic, hose with brown shoes, and red cloke are the colors he wears in the Bayeux Tapestry, where he sits on a red and gold throne

The first Great Seal of Edward the Confessor, 1059

Edward the Confessor
Slept under the dresser.
When that began to pall
He slept in the hall.
—E. C. Bently,
Biography for Beginners

King Edward the Confessor
1042 - 1066

Ever full of cheer was the blameless king,
Though for long in the past, deprived of his land,
He had trodden an exile's path across the wide world.
After Cnut had conquered the race of Aethelred,
And Danes ruled over this dear land
Of England for twenty-eight years
All told, squandering its riches.
In time he succeeded; noble in armor,
A king of excellent virtues, pure and benign,
Edward the noble protected his fatherland,
His realm and people: until suddenly came
That bitter death, which took so cruelly
The prince from the earth. Angels bore his
Righteous soul within Heaven's light.
Yet did the wise king entrust his kingdom
To a man of high rank, to Harold himself,
The noble earl, who ever
Faithfully obeyed his noble lord
In words and deeds, neglecting nothing
Whereof the national king stood in need.

—*The Anglo-Saxon Chronicle* for 1066

King Harold Godwinson
1066

Brown hair; gold and red crown; gold tunic; purple mantle; red hose; brown shoes; Haley's Comet (which will be back again in 1984), bringing the bad omen, gold and red; gold, red and green throne and palace; gold and red birds; white phantom invasion ships

From the Bayeux Tapestry

Earl Harold succeeded to the kingdom of England as the king granted it to him and as he was elected thereto.

—*The Anglo Saxon Chronicle*

King 'Arold came oop as they landed,
'Is face full of venom and 'ate,
'E said, "If you've come for Regatta,
You've got 'ere just six weeks too late."

King 'Arold 'e won the advantage,
On the 'illtop 'e took oop 'is stand,
With his knaves and 'is cads all around 'im,
On 'is 'orse with 'is 'awk in 'is 'and.

When the Conqueror saw
what 'ad 'appened,
A bow and an arrow 'e drew;
'E went right oop to 'Arold
and shot 'im,
'E were offside, but what
could they do?

And after the battle was over,
They found 'Arold so stately and grand,
Sitting there with an eye full of arrow,
On 'is 'orse with 'is 'awk in 'is 'and.

—Marriott Edgar, *The Battle of Hastings,*
(an old British music hall recitation piece)

William the Conqueror
1066 - 1087
From the Bayeux Tapestry

Gilt rim and bands of helmet and nosepiece, dark brown iron inner sections of helmet; coif and shirt of mail; white metal with a gilt colored rectangle across the chest— a sort of extra protection, probably, and gold stripes and circles at the bottom of the mail shirt; gold hose, brown horse with gold harness; gold mane, tail and stirrups; gold saddle edge with brown seat.

← Among other things we must not forget the good order he kept in the land, so that a man of any substance could travel unmolested through the country with his bosom full of gold. No man dared to slay another, no matter what evil the other might have done him. . . . He ruled over England, and by his foresight it was surveyed so carefully that there was not a hide of land in England of which he did not know who held it and how much it was worth.

—*The Anglo-Saxon Chronicle*

Very red face, grey eyes, yellow hair; gold crown with jewels and crimson lining; gold fibula or brooch; steel sword with gilt pommel; crimson mantle; silver background as this is taken from a silver penny and the description of Orderic Vitalis

William II Rufus

From a silver penny of William II

← He was of just stature, ordinary corpulence, fierce countenance; his forehead was bare of hair; of such great strength of arm, that it was often a matter of surprise, that no one was able to draw his bow, which himself could bend when his horse was on full gallop; he was majestic whether sitting or standing, although the protuberance of his belly deformed his royal person . . .

—William of Malmesbury, *Historia Anglorum.*

How Robert then, his eldest sonne, abroad,
Rufus, his second, seiz'd on his estate,
His father's steps apparently that trode,
Depressing those who had been conquer'd late:
But as on them he layd a heavie load,
So was he guerdon'd by impartiall fate;
For whilst men's roomes for beasts he did intend,
He in that forrest had a beastly end.

—Michael Drayton, *The Barons' Warres*

He was, when abroad, and in public assemblies, of supercilious look, darting his threatening eye on the by-stander; and with assumed severity and ferocious voice, assailing such as conversed with him. From apprehension of poverty, and of the treachery of others, as may be conjectured, he was too much given to lucre, and to cruelty. At home and at table, with his intimate companions, he gave loose to levity and to mirth. He was a most facetious railer at any thing he had himself done amiss, in order that he might thus do away with obloquy, and make it matter of jest . . .

—William of Malmesbury, *Historia Anglorum*

On Whit Sunday of this year [1099] at a village in Berkshire blood was seen bubbling forth from the ground, as many reported who were said to have seen it. And thereafter, on the morning after Lammas, King William was killed with an arrow while hunting by one of his men. He was afterwards brought to Winchester, and buried in the cathedral in the thirteenth year of his reign.

He was very harsh and fierce in his rule over his realm, and towards his followers and to all his neighbors, and very terrifying. Influenced by the advice of evil councillors, which was always agreeable to him, and by his own covetousness, he was continually exasperating this nation with depredations and unjust taxes. In his days, therefore, righteousness declined, and evil of every kind towards God and man put up its head. He oppressed the Church of God; and in his days when the head of a bishopric or an abbacy died, he either sold them all for money, or kept them within his grasp and let them for rent, for he claimed to be the heir of every man, cleric or lay.

—*Anglo-Saxon Chronicle*

Very red face, grey eyes, light yellow hair; gold crown and edging on tunic and mantle; white tunic and crimson mantle and shoes.

William II (Rufus) 1087 - 1100

From the description of Orderic and William of Malmesbury

King Henry I 1100 - 1135

After the effigy at Rochester

Henry, his young'st, his brother William dead,
Taketh the crowne from his usurping hand,
Due to the eldest, good Duke Robert's head,
Not then returned from the Holy Land;
Whose power was there so much diminished,
That he his foe not able to withstand,
Was ta'en in battell, and his eyes out-done;
For which, the seas left Henry not a sonne.
—Michael Drayton, *The Barons' Warres*

. . . King Henry held it as life's whole gain
That after his death, his son should reign . . .
King Henry of England's realm was he,
And Henry Duke of Normandy. . . .
Of ruthless strokes full many an one
He had struck to crown himself and his son;
And his elder brother's eyes were gone . . .

'Your son and all his fellowship
Lie low in the sea with the White Ship,'
King Henry fell as a man struck dead;
And speechless still he stared from his bed
When to him next day my rede I read.
There's many an hour must needs beguile
A King's high heart that he should smile—
Full many a lordly hour, full fain
Of his realm's rule and pride of his reign—
But this King never smiled again . . .
—Dante Gabriel Rossetti, "The White Ship"

Dark hair; gold crown, sceptre and tunic under a white silken damaltic edged with gold and gems. Brightly-colored mantle, lined with black sables, fastened with a gold ring.

King Stephen 1135 - 1154

To Maud the Empresse he [Henry I] the scepter leaves,
His onely daughter, whom (through false pretext)
Stephen, Earle of Bulloyn, from the kingdome heaves:
The conqueror's nephew, in succession next,
By which, the land a stranger warre receives,
Wherewith it long was miserably vext;
Till Stephen fayling, and his issue gone,
The heir of Maud steps up into the throne.

—Michael Drayton, *The Barons' Warres*

From the second Great Seal of Stephen, 1144

The Phrygian helmet: gilt framework, blue-grey metal inner sections; hauberk and coif of mail: blue-grey; crimson shield and cross pattee on white field of flag; crimson and white streamers; crimson horse trappings and spur harness, brass fittings.

Henry the second, Maud the Empresse sonne,
Of th' English kings, Plantaginet the first,
By Stephen's end, a glorious reigne begun;
But yet his greatnesse strangely was accurst,
By his sonne Henrie's coronation;
Which to his age much woe and sorrow nurst;
When his, whom he had labor'd to make great,
Abroad his townes, at home usurp'd his seat.

—Michael Drayton, *The Barons' Warres*

He was somewhat red of face, and broad-breasted; short of body, and therewithal fat, which made him use much exercise, and little meat. He was commonly called Henry Short-mantle, because he was the first that brought the use of short cloaks out of Anjou into England. Concerning endowments of mind, he was of a spirit in the highest degree generous; which made him often say, that all the world sufficed not to a courageous heart. His custom was to be always in action; for which cause, if he had no real wars, he would have feigned; and would transport forces either into Normandy or Britanny, and go with them himself, whereby he was always prepared of an army; and made it a schooling to his soldiers, and to himself an exercise. To his children he was both indulgent and hard; for out of indulgence he caused his son Henry to be crowned King in his own time; and out of hardness he caused his younger sons to rebel against him.

—Sir Richard Baker,
A Chronicle of the Kings of England

To the Patriarch of Jerusalem, who urged him to go on Crusade: "If I should be absent out of my kingdom, my own sons would be ready to rise up against me in my absence." They did.

—Baker

In an outburst of rage against Thomas a Becket, his Archbishop of Canterbury: "Shall I never be at quiet for this priest? If I had any about me that loved me, they would find some way or other to rid me of this trouble." Four of his knights took this broad hint and murdered Becket in his own cathedral.

—Baker

Ruddy face, reddish, curly hair; gold crown and sceptre; crimson dalmatic, or tunic, with gold edging, over an under-tunic of blue with a gold border, and under this a white garment, the alb. Dark brown mantle with gold border and white lining; white gloves, green shoes with gold bands and gold spurs with red straps.

Henry II 1154 - 1189

After the effigy at Fontevrault

Richard, his sonne, him worthily succeeds;
Who not content with what was safely ours,
(A man whose mind sought after glorious deeds)
Into the east transports the English powers;
Where, with his sword, while many a pagan bleeds,
Relentless fate doth haste on his last houres,
By one, whose syre he justly there had slaine,
With a sharpe arrow shot into the braine.
—Michael Drayton, *The Barons' Warres*

No-one will tell me the cause of my sorrow,
Why they have made me a prisoner here.
Wherefore with dolor I now make my moan;
Friends had I many but help have I none.
Shameful it is that they leave me to ransom,
To languish here two winters long.
—Richard I, from a poem written while he was held prisoner in Austria, on his way home from the Crusade

Richard, 6 feet 2 inches tall, had hair somewhere between yellow and red, and bright blue eyes. Damaltic: red silk, white lining, gold borders; green under-tunic with gold borders; below, a white alb. Mantle: blue with gold border and jeweled clasp; red shoes with gold bands, gold spurs with black straps.

Adapted from the effigy at Fontevrault

Richard the Lionhearted
1189 - 1199

Next followed him his faithlesse brother John,
By Arthur's murther (compass'd by his might)
His brother Geffrey, th 'Earle of Britaines' sonne;
But he by poyson was repay'd his spight;
For whilst he strove to have made all his owne,
(For what he got by wrong, he held his right)
And on the clergie tyrannously fed,
Was by a monke of Winsted poysoned.

—Michael Drayton, *The Barons' Warres*

King John was not a good king . . .

—A. A. Milne

Reddish hair; jeweled gold crown; crimson tunic with gold edging and jeweled collar and sleeves; crimson belt with jewels; gold under-tunic; red hose; gold spurs with blue straps; black shoes and white gloves. Crimson scabbard and gilt sword pommel and fittings.

After the effigy in Worcester Cathedral

King John
1199 - 1216

From the effigy by Wm. Torel, Westminster Abbey

Henry his sonne, then crowned very young,
For hate the English to the father bare,
The sonne's here raigning was in question long,
Who thought, on France t'have cast the kingdomes' care:
With whom the Barons, insolent and strong,
For the old charter in commotion were;
Which his long raigne did with much care molest,
Yet with much peace went lastly to his rest.

—Michael Drayton, *The Barons' Warres*

Henry III 1216 - 1272

He was of stature but mean, yet of a well compacted body, and very strong; one of his eyelids hanging down, and almost covering the black of his eye; for his inward endowments, it may be said, he was wiser for a man, than for a prince; for he knew better how to govern his life than his subjects. He was rather pious than devout, as taking more pleasure in hearing masses than sermons; as he once said to the King of France, he had rather see his friend once, than hear from him often. His mind seemed not to stand firm upon its basis, for every sudden accident put him into passion. He was neither constant in his love, nor in his hate; for he never had so great a favorite whom he cast not into disgrace, nor so great an enemy whom he received not into favor.

—Sir Richard Baker,
A Chronicle of the Kings of England

Auburn hair; gold crown; green mantle with gold edging and gold and jeweled clasp; crimson surcote over gold tunic; and crimson shoes.

Of him descends a prince, stout, just, and sage,
(In all things happie, but in him, his sonne)
In whom, wise Nature did her selfe ingage,
More than in man, in Edward to have done;
Whose happie raigne recur'd the former rage,
By the large bounds he to his empire wonne:
O God (quoth he [Edward II]) had he my patterne bin,
Heav'n had not pour'd these plagues upon my sinne.

—Michael Drayton, *The Barons' Warres*

He was tall of stature, higher than ordinary men by head and shoulders, and thereof called Longshank: of a swarthy complexion, strong of body, but lean; of a comely favor; his eyes in his anger, sparkling like fire; the hair of his head black and curled. Concerning his conditions, as he was in war peaceful; so in peace he was warlike, delighting specially in that kind of hunting, which is to kill stags or other wild beasts with spears. In continency of life, he was equal to his father; in acts of valor, far beyond him. He had in him the two wisdoms, not often found in any, single; both together, seldom or never: an ability of judgment in himself, and a readiness to hear the judgment of others. He was not easily provoked into passion, but once in passion, not easily appeased, as was seen by his dealing with the Scots; towards whom he showed at first patience, and at last severity. If he be censured for his many taxations, he may be justified by his well bestowing them; for never prince laid out his money to more honor of himself, or good of his kingdom. His great unfortunateness was in his greatest blessing; for of four sons which he had by his wife Queen Eleanor, three of them died in his own life time, who were worthy to have outlived him; and the fourth outlived him, who was worthy never to have been born.

—Sir Richard Baker,
A Chronicle of the Kings of England

Edward I wore simple clothes, and seldom his crown. Brown hair; gold crown and sceptre; red tunic, black belt, red hose; rose-colored mantle.

Edward I
1272 - 1307

From a statue of Edward I on the tomb of John Eltham, Westminster Abby

From the effigy in Gloucester Cathedral

Edward II
1307 - 1327

I must have wanton poets, pleasant wits,
Musicians, that with touching of a string
May draw the pliant king which way I please.
Music and poetry is his delight;
Therefore I'll have Italian masks by night,
Sweet speeches, comedies, and pleasing shows;
And in the day, when he shall walk abroad,
Like sylvan nymphs my pages shall be clad;
My men, like satyrs grazing on the lawns,
Shall with their goat-feet dance the antic hay.
Sometime a lovely boy in Dian's shape,
With hair that gilds the water as it glides,
Crownets of pearl about his naked arms,
And in his sportful hands an olive-tree,
To hide those parts which men delight to see,
Shall bathe him in a spring; and there hard by,
One like Actaeon peeping through the grove,
Shall by the angry goddess be transformed,
And running in the likeness of an hart
By yelping hounds pulled down,
shall seem to die: —
Such things as these best please his majesty.

—Christopher Marlowe,
King Edward II: Edward's favorite.
Piers Gaveston, is speaking.

But when I call to mind I am a king,
Methinks I should revenge me of my wrongs,
That Mortimer and Isabel have done.
But what are kings, when regiment is gone,
But perfect shadows in a sunshine day?
I wear the crown, but am controlled by them,
By Mortimer, and my unconstant queen,
Who spots my nuptial bed with infamy . . .

—Marlowe, *Edward II*

The dungeon where they keep me is the sink
Wherein the filth of all the castle falls.
. . .
And there in mire and puddle have I stood
This ten days' space; and,
lest that I should sleep,
One plays continually upon a drum.
They give me bread and water, being a king;
So that, for want of sleep and sustenance,
My mind's distempered,
and my body's numbed
And whether I have limbs or no I know not.
O, would my blood dropped
out from every vein,
As doth this water from my tattered robes.
Tell Isabel, the queen, I looked not thus,
When for her sake I ran at tilt in France,
And there unhorsed the Duke of Cleremont.

—Marlowe, *Edward II*

Brown hair; gold crown,
sceptre and orb; red tunic and shoes; brown mantle.

From the Treatise of Walter de Milemete,
De Nobilitatibus Sapientiis, Christ Church Library, Oxford

Young Edward III, 1327

Light brown hair; red robe, brown gloves and shoes; gilt chair and arch.

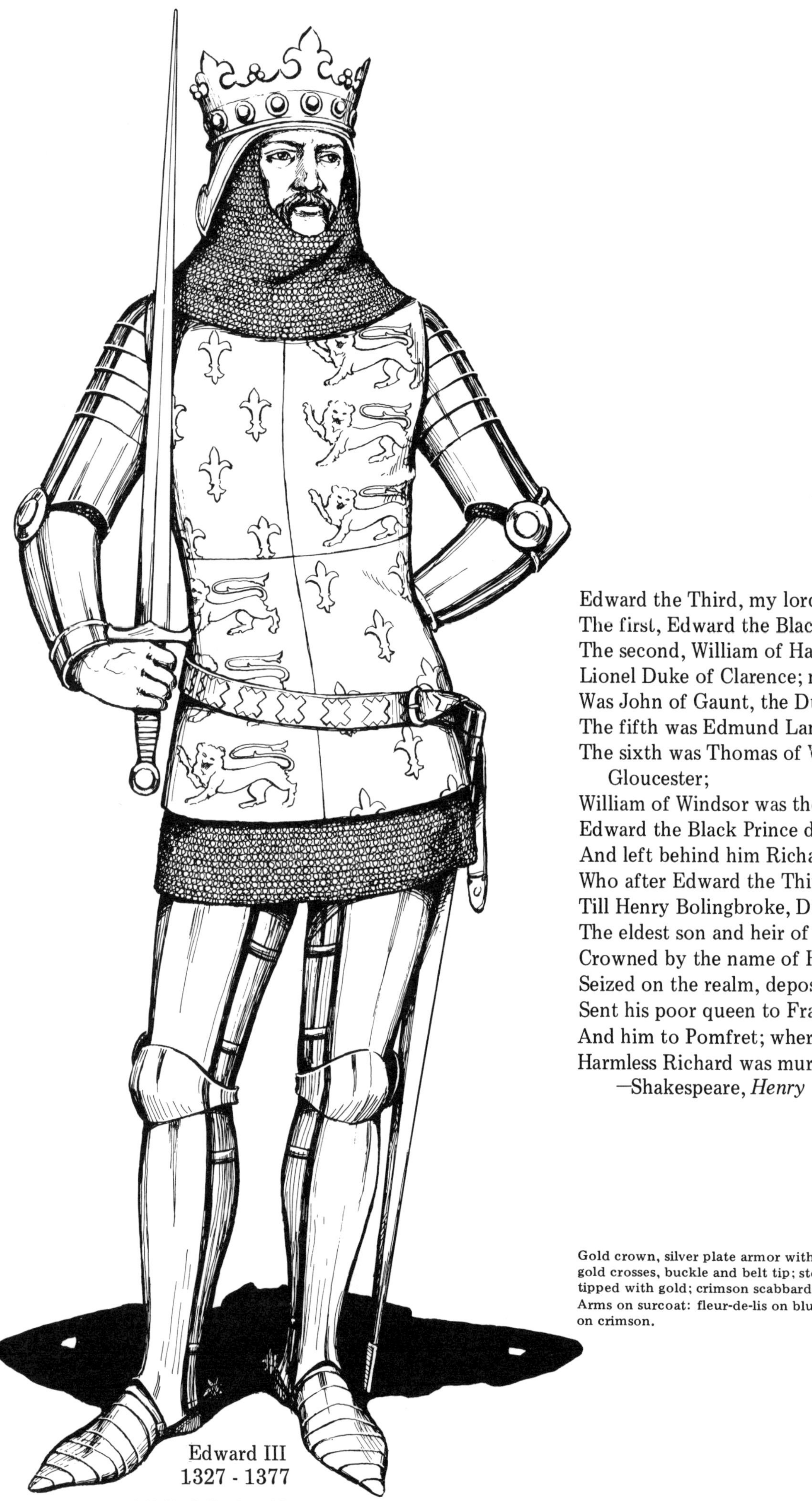

Edward III
1327 - 1377

From the brass of Sir Hugh Hastings, Elsyng, Norfolk, 1347

Edward the Third, my lords, had seven sons:
The first, Edward the Black Prince, Prince of Wales;
The second, William of Hatfield; and the third,
Lionel Duke of Clarence; next to whom
Was John of Gaunt, the Duke of Lancaster;
The fifth was Edmund Langley, Duke of York;
The sixth was Thomas of Woodstock, Duke of
Gloucester;
William of Windsor was the seventh and last.
Edward the Black Prince died before his father
And left behind him Richard, his only son,
Who after Edward the Third's death reigned as king;
Till Henry Bolingbroke, Duke of Lancaster,
The eldest son and heir of John of Gaunt,
Crowned by the name of Henry the Fourth,
Seized on the realm, deposed the rightful king,
Sent his poor queen to France, from whence she came
And him to Pomfret; where, as all you know,
Harmless Richard was murdered traitorously.
—Shakespeare, *Henry VI, Part II*

Gold crown, silver plate armor with gilt edging; crimson belt with gold crosses, buckle and belt tip; steel sword with crimson pommel tipped with gold; crimson scabbard tipped with gilt material. Royal Arms on surcoat: fleur-de-lis on blue (azure); gold (or) leopards on crimson.

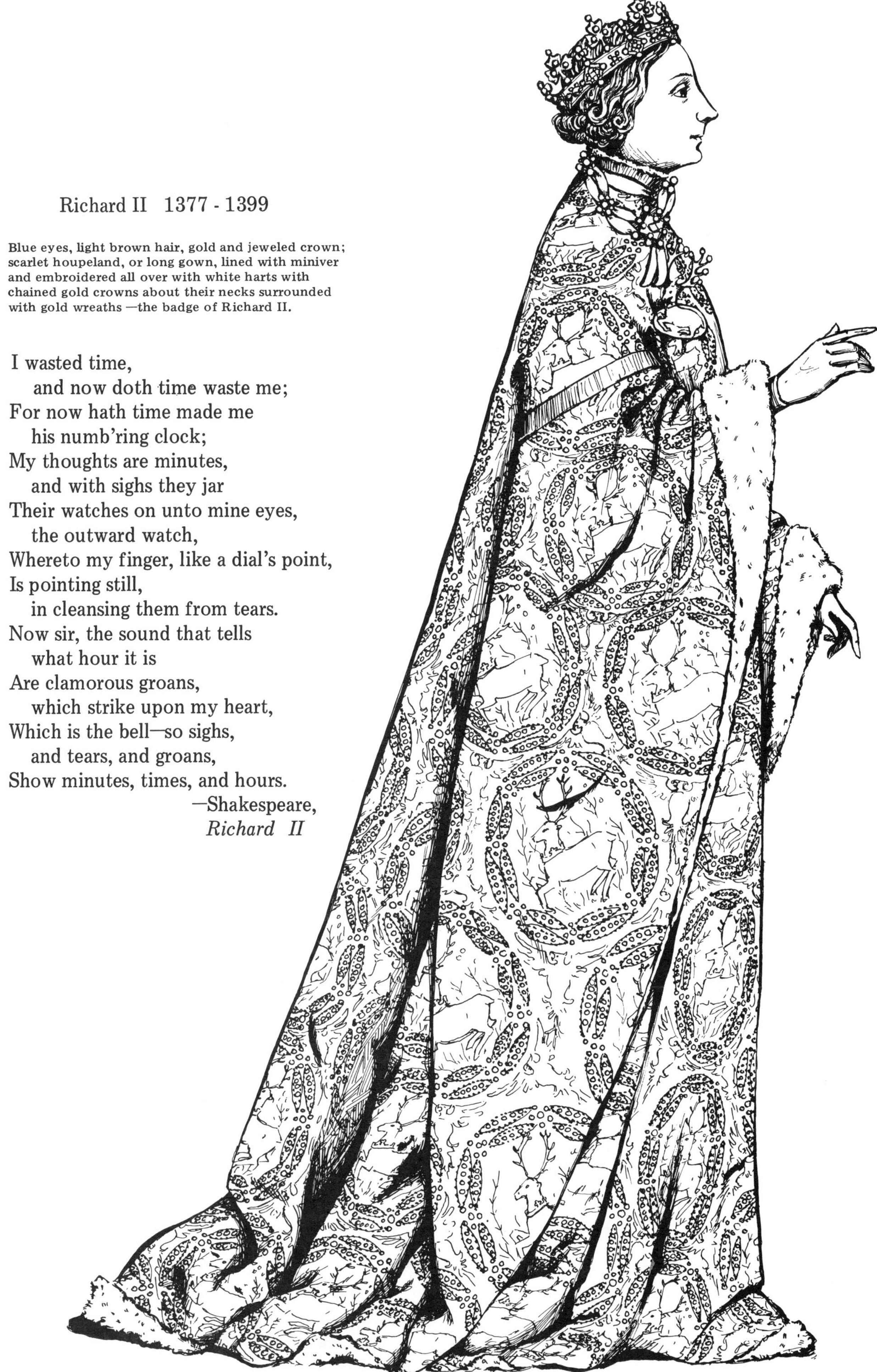

Richard II 1377 - 1399

Blue eyes, light brown hair, gold and jeweled crown; scarlet houpeland, or long gown, lined with miniver and embroidered all over with white harts with chained gold crowns about their necks surrounded with gold wreaths —the badge of Richard II.

I wasted time,
and now doth time waste me;
For now hath time made me
his numb'ring clock;
My thoughts are minutes,
and with sighs they jar
Their watches on unto mine eyes,
the outward watch,
Whereto my finger, like a dial's point,
Is pointing still,
in cleansing them from tears.
Now sir, the sound that tells
what hour it is
Are clamorous groans,
which strike upon my heart,
Which is the bell—so sighs,
and tears, and groans,
Show minutes, times, and hours.
—Shakespeare,
Richard II

From the Wilton Diptich, 1382; National Gallery, London

Henry IV 1399 - 1413

From the effigy in Canterbury Cathedral

Uneasy lies the head
  that wears a crown.
. . . .
God knows, my son,
By what by-paths and
  indirect crook'd ways
I met this crown,
  and I myself know well
How troublesome it sat upon my head.
To thee it shall descend
  with better quiet,
Better opinion, better confirmation,
For all the soil of
  the achievement goes
With me into the earth.
  It seem'd in me
But as an honor snatch'd
  with boist'rous hand,
And I had many living to upbraid
My gain of it by their assistances,
Which daily grew to quarrel
  and to bloodshed,
Wounding supposed peace.
  All these bold fears
Thou seest with peril I have answered;
For all my reign hath been
  but as a scene
Acting that argument.
  And now my death
Changes the mood,
  for what in me was purchas'd
Falls upon thee in a more fairer sort;
So thou the garland wear'st successively.
. . . Therefore, my Harry,
Be it thy course to busy giddy minds
With foreign quarrels,
  that action hence borne out
May waste the memory of former days.

—William Shakespeare,
King Henry IV, Part 2

Brown hair, gold and jeweled crown, gold sceptre; green surcote and mantle —colors of his Order of the Bath, edged with gold and jewels.

Henry V
1413 - 1422

If we are mark'd to die, we are enow
To do our country loss; and if to live,
The fewer men, the greater share of honor.
God's will! I pray thee, wish not one man more.
By Jove, I am not covetous for gold,
Nor care I who doth feed upon my cost;
It earns me not if men my garments wear;
Such outward things dwell not in my desires;
But if it be a sin to covet honor,
I am the most offending soul alive.
No, faith, my coz, wish not a man from England:
God's peace! I would not lose so great an honor
As one man more, methinks, would share from me,
For the best hope I have. O do not wish one more!
Rather proclaim it, Westmoreland, through my host,
That he which hath no stomach to this fight,
Let him depart; his passport shall be made,
And crowns for convoy put into his purse:
We would not die in that man's company
That fears his fellowship to die with us.
This day is call'd the feast of Crispian:
He that outlives this day, and comes safe home,
Will stand a tip-toe when this day is nam'd,
And rouse him at the name of Crispian.
He that shall see this day, and live old age,
Will yearly on the vigil feast his neighbors,
And say, 'To-morrow is Saint Crispian':
Then will he strip his sleeve and show his scars,
And say, 'These wounds I had on Crispin's day.'
Old men forget; yet all shall be forgot,
But he'll remember with advantages
What feats he did that day . . .
This story shall the good man teach his son;
And Crispin Crispian shall ne'er go by,
From this day to the ending of the world,
But we in it shall be remembered;
We few, we happy few, we band of brothers;
For he to-day that sheds his blood with me
Shall be my brother; be he ne'er so vile
This day shall gentle his condition:
And gentlemen in England now a-bed
Shall think themselves accurs'd they were not here,
And hold their manhoods cheap whiles any speaks
That fought with us upon Saint Crispin's day.

—William Shakespeare, *King Henry V:*
the king's speech before
the battle of Agincourt

Brown eyes and hair, ruddy complexion; gold and jeweled chain; gold brocade undergown, crimson slashed sleeves, brown fur-trimmed tabard or gown.

From a portrait in the Royal Collection

Henry VI
1422 - 1471

From a portrait in the Royal Collection

Was ever king that joy'd an earthly throne,
And could command no more content than I?
No sooner was I crept out of my cradle
But I was made a king at nine months old.
Was never subject long'd to be a king
As I do long and wish to be a subject.
—William Shakespeare, *King Henry VI, Part 2*

O God! methinks it were a happy life
To be no better than a homely swain;
To sit upon a hill, as I do now,
To carve out dials quaintly, point by point,
Thereby to see the minutes how they run—
How many makes the hour full complete,
How many hours brings about the day,
How many days will finish up the year,
How many years a mortal man may live,
When this is known, then to divide the times—
So many hours must I tend my flock;
So many hours must I take my rest;
So many hours must I contemplate;
So many hours must I sport myself;
So many days my ewes have been with young;
So many weeks ere the poor fools will ean;
So many years ere I shall shear the fleece;
So minutes, hours, days, weeks, months, and years,
Pass'd over to the end they were created,
Would bring white hairs unto a quiet grave,
Ai, what a life were this! how sweet! how lovely!
—William Shakespeare, *King Henry VI, Part 3:*
King Henry is soliloquizing as he sits
on a hillside above a battle where men fight
to see whether he will remain king.

Kingdoms are but cares,
State is devoid of stay,
Riches are ready snares,
And hasten to decay.
Pleasure is a privy prick
Which vice doth still provoke;
Pomp, imprompt; and fame, a flame;
Power, a smoldering smoke,
Who meaneth to remove the rock
Out of the slimy mud,
Shall mire himself, and hardly 'scape
The swelling of the flood,
—Henry VI: written while
a prisoner in the Tower of London

Brown hair and eyes; black bonnet; gold and jeweled chain and cross; gold rings; gold collar of undergarment; crimson sleeves trimmed with brown fur; black tabard or gown, edged with white ermine.

Having defeated the Lancastrians and had children to inherit the throne, Edward thought he had established the Yorkist dynasty.

Young Ned, for thee thine uncles and myself
Have in our armours watch'd the winter's night,
Went all afoot in summer's scalding heat,
That thou might'st repossess the crown in peace;
And of our labors thou shalt reap the gain,

—William Shakespeare, *King Henry VI, Part 3;*
Edward is speaking to his son,
who reigned briefly as Edward V.

Edward IV 1461 - 1483

Brown hair, black bonnet; gold brocade gown with black pattern, lined with ermine; black undergarment with strings of pearls and gold and jeweled pendants; gold belt.

Adapted from a portrait in the Royal Collection

Edward V 1483

In *King Richard III*, when Richard, the boy-king's uncle, suggests he will be safest in the royal palace at the Tower of London, Shakespeare has Edward answer:

"I do not like the Tower, of any place."

Edward was taken there with his young brother, and the two of them were never seen again. Most think they were killed by order of their uncle Richard; some believe that the villain was not Richard, but their brother-in-law, Henry VII.

Edward IV has brown hair; Edward V and his mother have yellow hair. Gold crowns, sceptres and orb; blue gowns and crimson mantles edged with ermine.

Edward IV, Edward V and Queen Elizabeth
From Lambeth Palace MS 265

Richard III 1483 - 1485

And yet I know not how to get the crown,
For many lives stand between me and home;
And I, like one lost in a thorny wood,
That rents the thorns and is rent with
the thorns,
Seeking a way, and straying from the way;
Not knowing how to find the open air,
But toiling desperately to find it out—
Torment myself to catch the English crown:
And from that torment I will free myself,
Or hew my way out with a bloody axe.
Why, I can smile, and murder whiles I smile,
And cry 'Content!' to that that grieves
my heart,
And wet my cheeks with artificial tears,
And frame my face to all occasions.
. . .
I can add colors to the chameleon,
Change shapes with Proteus for advantages,
And set the murderous Machiavel to school.
Can I do this, and cannot get a crown!
Tut! were it further off, I'll pluck it down.
—William Shakespeare, *King Henry VI, Part 3:*
here Richard first discusses his plans.

But I, that am not shaped for sportive tricks,
Nor made to court an amorous looking-glass;
I, that am rudely stampt, and want love's
majesty
To strut before a wanton ambling nymph;
I, that am curtail'd of this fair proportion,
Cheated of feature by dissembling nature,
Deform'd, unfinisht, sent before my time
Into this breathing world, scarce half made up,
And that so lamely and unfashionable
That dogs bark at me as I halt by them;—
Why, I, in this weak piping time of peace,
Have no delight to pass away the time,
Unless to spy my shadow in the sun,
And descant on mine own deformity:
And therefore, since I cannot prove a lover,
To entertain these fair well-spoken days,
I am determined to prove a villain,
And hate the idle pleasures of these days.
—Shakespeare, *King Richard III*

Brown hair, grey eyes; black bonnet with a gold and jeweled hat pin; gold tunic showing at the collar, chest below a crimson undergarment, and through slit sleeves of a black gown which is lined with ermine; gold rings, black hose, red shoes.

Adapted from a portrait in the National Portrait Gallery, London

Henry VII: grey eyes, a wart on his cheek, brown hair with entwined red and white roses; gold brocade pourpoint underdress edged and caught together with lace; crimson outer robe called a simar, with ermine.

Henry VII and Elizabeth of York, from a medallion struck to commemorate their marriage, 1486

Queen Elizabeth of York: gold and jewelled crown, yellow hair, a "kyrtle (or jacket or bodice) of white cloth of gold damask, and a mantle of the same suit, furred with ermine;"

Henry VII 1485 - 1509

And then, as we have ta'en the sacrament,
We will unite the white rose and the red.
Smile heaven upon this fair conjunction,
That long have frown'd upon their enmity!—
What traitor hears me, and says not Amen?
England hath long been mad and scarr'd herself;
The brother blindly shed the brother's blood,
The father rashly slaughter'd his own son,
The son, compell'd, been butcher to the sire:
All this divided York and Lancaster,
Divided in their dire division,
O now let Richmond and Elizabeth,
The true succeeders of each royal house,
By God's fair ordinance conjoin together!
And let their heirs—God, if Thy will be so—
Enrich the time to come with smooth-faced peace,
With smiling plenty, and fair prosperous days!

—William Shakespeare, *King Richard III:* after defeating Richard, Henry makes this speech as he takes the throne.

Bright white steel armor; gold crown; red and white plumes (perhaps); shield of arms and caparisons: white fleurs-de-lis on blue; gold leopards on red; red crosses; color the greyhound as you like; blue sky; green grass. You might enjoy HENRY VIII & HIS WIVES—PAPER DOLLS, just $2.50 at your store or museum or add 50c for shipping and write us.

The third Great Seal of Henry VIII, 1544

Henry VIII 1509 - 1547

In the Tower o'London, large as life,
The ghost of Anne Boelyn walks, they declare;
For Anne Boelyn was once King 'Enry's wife
Until 'e made the 'eadsman bob 'er 'air.
Ah, yes, 'e did 'er wrong long years ago,
And she comes up at night to tell 'im so.
With 'er 'ead tucked
Underneath 'er arm,
She walks the Bloody Tower,
With 'er 'ead tucked
Underneath 'er arm,
At the midnight hour,
She comes to 'aunt King 'Enry,
She means giving 'im what for,
Gadzooks! She's going to tell 'im off
For 'aving spilled her gore;
And just in case the 'eadsman wants
To give 'er an encore,
She 'as 'er 'ead tucked
Underneath 'er arm.
With 'er 'ead tucked
Underneath 'er arm,
She walks the Bloody Tower;
With 'er 'ead tucked
Underneath 'er arm,
At the midnight hour.

—R. P. Weston and Burt Lee,
"With 'Er 'Ead Tucked
Underneath 'er Arm,"
a popular English musichall song.

Edward VI 1547 - 1553

From the portrait in the National Portrait Gallery, London

The yere of our Lord 1537, was a prince born to king harry th' eight, by Jane Seymour, when quene, who w'in few days after the Birth of her soone died, and was buried at the castel of Windwore. This child was christened by the duke of Northfolke, the duke of Southfolke, and the archbishop of Caunterbury. Afterward was brought up till he came to six yeres old among the women. At the sixt yere of his age, he was brought up in learning by Mr. Doctour Cox who was after his amner [almoner], and Jhon Cheke, Mr. of Arts, tow wel learned men, who sought to bring him up in learning of toungues, of the scripture, of philosophie, and all liberal sciences. Also John Belmaine frenchman did teach him the french language. The 10 yere not yet ended, it was apointed he should be created prince of Wales, Duke of Cornwal, and Conte Palatine of Chester. At wich time, being the year of our L. 1547 the said king died of a dropsie as it was thought. After whos death incontinent came Edward erle of Hartford, and S. Antony Brown, Mr. of the horse, to convey this prince to Enfild, where the earle of Hertford declared to him and his younger Sister Elizabeth, the death of their father.

—from Edward's chronicle of his own time, written when he was 12½: English spelling was not to be standardized for another two hundred years, so Edward's teachers are not to be blamed for leaving him ignorant.

Light brown hair; black velvet cap with white plume; black doublet and breeches; black lower sleeves. Crimson coat with white ermine fur lining and collar. Gold lace on puffed sleeves edged with pearls. White stockings; crimson shoes.

Queen Mary 1553 - 1558

And now, good subjects, pluck up your hearts, and like true men, stand fast against these rebels, both our enemies and yours, and fear them not, for I assure you I fear them nothing at all.
—Queen Mary's speech at the Guildhall, to rally London's support against Wyatt's rebellion.

"When I am dead and opened, you shall find 'Calais' lying in my heart."
—Rafael Holinshed's *Chronicle*

Light reddish brown hair; red velvet cap with black and white edging; white pearls alternating with red stones. Black veil. Red and gold brocade gown; white trim around neck and bottom of underskirt. White pearls. Crimson velvet cuffs and underskirt. White undersleeves with black edging. Girdle or waistbelt and trim on underskirt: pearls alternating with red and black stones in gilt settings.

Adapted from a portrait in the National Portrait Gallery, London

Young Queen Elizabeth I 1558 - 1603

Exchequer Seal of Elizabeth I, 1563

I assure you, I do not desire to live to distrust my faithful and loving people. Let tyrants fear. I have always so behaved myself that, under God, I have placed my chiefest strength and safeguard in the loyal hearts and goodwill of my subjects; and therefore I am come amongst you, as you see, at this time, not for my recreation and disport, but being resolved, in the midst and heat of battle, to live or die amongst you all, to lay down for my God, and for my kingdom, and for my people, my honor and my blood, even in the dust. I know I have the body of a weak and feeble woman, but I have the heart and stomach of a king, and of a king of England too, and I think foul scorn that Parma, or Spain, or any prince of Europe should dare to invade the borders of my realm. . . .

—Elizabeth's speech to her troops at Tilbury, before the Armada

I am your annointed Queen. I will never be by violence constrained to do anything. I thank God I am endued with such qualities that if I were turned out of the Realm in my petticoat I were able to live in any place in Christendom.

—Elizabeth

Light red hair; headpiece, red with black and white decoration, with pearls. Large red stone at point with white pearl on top. Jewels in hair: pearls. Black stones in gilt setting; red and black jeweled globe near left ear. Pearl necklace. Black stone in center front, red stones on sides, settings gilt. White lace collar and cuffs, white dress. Center of rosettes: gilt, with either pearls, red or black stones. Gold fan with black pieces, pearls set in red circles. Red ribbon attached to dress. Tan leather gloves.

Opposite: red hair; gold crown (with crimson lining); gold sceptre, orb and cross; gold brocade dalmatic over an alb of white silk; crimson mantle with an ermine cape; red and white Tudor roses; white fleurs-de-lis against blue; gilt chair, canopy, baldachino and pillars; crimson curtains; this is from a bronze-green seal in the British Museum. Gilt lines and mullets.

When I was fair and young
 And favor graced me,
Of many was I sought their
 Mistress for to be,
But I did scorn them all and
 Answered them therefore,
Go, go, go, seek
 Some other where,
Importune me no more.

—from a poem by Elizabeth

Queen Elizabeth I

National Portrait Gallery, London

James I 1603 - 1625

Dark brown hair; white collar, doublet, breeches, hose and shoes. Gilt buttons. Crimson velvet robe lined with ermine white fur; gold lace edging. Cord and tassels: crimson and gold. Garter collar: dark blue circled garters with gold edging and letters. Bows, gold. Red rose in center of garters. Sword belt: gilt with pearls and various colored precious stones. Gilt sword. Gold orb and sceptre. Gold crown with pearls and various colored precious stones over crimson velvet. Garter on knee: dark blue with gold edging and letters.

. . . He knew that those who would
with love command
Must with a tender (yet a steadfast) hand
Sustain the reins, and in the Check forbear
To offer cause of injury, or fear;
That kings, by their example,
more do sway
Than by their power; and men do
more obey
When they are led, than when
they are compelled.
In all these knowing arts
our Prince excelled . . .

—Ben Jonson, from "A Penegyre, on the Happie Entrance of James, Our Soveraigne, to His first high session of Parliament"

After Paul van Somer, Royal Collection

Fresh as the Day, and new as are the Hours,
Our first of fruits, that is the prime of flowers
Bred by your breath, on this low bank of ours;
Now, in a garland by the graces knit:
Upon this obelisk, advanced for it,
We offer as a Circle the most fit
To crown the years, which you begin,
great king,
And you, with them, as father of our spring.
—Ben Jonson,
"A Song of Welcome to King Charles"

Charles I 1625 - 1649
After Van Dyke, Royal Collection

Charles's early popularity did not last. Eventually he was put on trial before Parliament, whose power over him he refused to acknowledge. They condemned him to death, but he expressed his political opinions in a final speech before being beheaded January 30, 1649: "For the People . . . I must tell you that their Liberty and Freedom consists in having the Government of those Laws, by which the Life and their Goods may be most their own; 'tis not for having share in Government, that is nothing pertaining to 'em. A Subject and a Sovereign are clean different things."

Dark brown hair; lace collar, cuffs, boot tops, all white. Doublet and breeches: crimson velvet with gold silk stripes and trim. Yellow ribbons at waist of doublet. Gilt buttons. Ribbon worn over shoulders with medallion: Royal Blue. Gold medallion. Gloves and boots: light tan leather. Black hat with yellow ribbons. Stick: reddish-brown wood.

He came with a triumph of over twenty thousand horse and foot brandishing their swords and shouting with inexpressible joy. The ways were strewn with flowers, the bells were ringing, the streets were hung with tapestry, and the fountains were running wine. The Mayor, Aldermen, and all the Companies, in their chains of gold, liveries, and banners, were present; also the lords and nobles. Everybody was clad in cloth of silver, gold, and velvet; the windows and balconies were all set with ladies, trumpets, and music, and myriads of people flocked the streets. . . .

—Sir John Evelyn, *Diary:* Evelyn is describing Charles's entry into London in 1660, when the monarchy was restored.

Providing for events to come,
When he resign'd the Throne,
Still he maintain'd his Kingly State;
And grew familiar with his fate.
Kind, good and gracious to the last,
On all he lov'd before, his dying beams he cast:
Oh truly good, and truly great,
For glorious as he rose benignly so he set!
. . .
Oh frail Estate of Human things,
And slippery hopes below!
Now to our Cost your Emptiness we know,
(For 'tis a lesson dearly bought)
Assurance here is never to be sought.
The Best, and best belov'd of Kings,
And best deserving to be so.
When scarce he had escap'd the fatal blow
Of Faction and Conspiracy,
Death did his promis'd hopes destroy:
He toyl'd, He gain'd, but liv'd not to enjoy.
What mists of Providence are these
Through which we cannot see!

—John Dryden, *Threnodia Augustalis*

Here lies a great and mighty king
Whose promise none relies on;
He never said a foolish thing,
Nor ever did a wise one.

—mock epitaph for Charles by his friend John Wilmot, Earl of Rochester.

Charles II
1660 - 1685
After J. M. Wright

Dark brown hair; dark blue cap, white plumes; white lace cravat; also white: hose, shirt, stockings. Robe: dark blue velvet. Sash: red velvet; white ribbon on shoulder. Lining of robe: white satin. Garter insignia: gold embroidery with red cross. Yellow cord with red and green; tassels are gold. Garter collar: gold with dark blue garters and red roses in center.

Blue eyes, dark brown hair; white neckcloth and shirt sleeves. Gold silk brocade oversleeves, yellow ribbons. Steel breast plate. Scarlet sash over shoulder. Brown leather tunic skirt; brown satin breeches. White ribbon ties at knees; brown shoes with white ribbons. Gilt baton.

James II 1685 - 1688

After Sir Peter Lely

A Warlike Prince ascends the Regal State,
A Prince, long exercis'd by Fate:
Long may he keep, tho' he obtains it late,
Heroes, in Heaven's peculiar Mold are cast,
They and their poets are not form'd in hast;
Man was the first in God's design, and Man was
made the last.
. . .
Long may they fear this awful Prince,
And not Provoke his lingring Sword;
Peace is their only sure Defence,
Their best Security his Word:
In all the Changes of his doubtful State,
His Truth, like Heav'ns, was kept inviolate,
For him to Promise is to make it Fate.
His Valor can Triumph o'r Land and Main;
With broken Oaths his Fame he will not stain;
With Conquest, Basely bought, and with
Inglorious gain.

—John Dryden, *Threnodia Augustalis*

Charles II had appointed Dryden as England's second poet laureate—a poet given a salary by the monarch, whose duty was to praise his ruler. Dryden did good service to Charles, and was inherited by James, who offered less material for a panegyrist. Dryden did his best, praising James's "warlike Mind, his Soul devoid of Fear, His High-designing Thoughts"; but most Englishmen concentrated more on James's defects, and within three years threw him out of the country.

WILLIAM III: dark brown hair, white cravat, black armor, gold sword belt. Light brown breeches, crimson robe lined with ermine, gilt baton. MARY II: dark brown hair, blue eyes, white head piece and pearl necklace. Emerald green satin dress with white lace trim, white sleeves. Gold brooch with red and green stones. Crimson and ermine robe.

Mary came in for her share of poetical eulogies:

By beauteous softness
 mixt with Majesty,
An Empire over every
 Heart she gains
And from her awful Powe
 none could be free,
She with such Sweetness
 and such Justice Reigns.
—T. Shadwell, Birthday Ode, 1689

William and Mary 1689 - 169
William III 1694 - 1702

After Wissing and Lely

When William and Mary came to power, Dryden was deprived of the Poet Laureateship, which was conferred on Shadwell, of whose verse Dryden had once commented that other poets "to some faint meaning make pretense. But Shadwell never deviates into sense." From this time on the Poets Laureate wrote annual odes praising the sovereign on his or her birthday and on New Year's Day, a custom that endured until the 1830's and led to some amazingly poor poetry.

Close by those meads, forever crowned with
flowers,
Where Thames with pride surveys his rising
towers,
There stands a structure of majestic frame,
Which from the neighboring Hampton
takes its name.
Here Britain's statesmen oft the fall foredoom
Of foreign tyrants and of nymphs at home;
Here thou, great Anna! whom three realms
obey,
Dost sometimes counsel take—and sometimes
tea.

—Alexander Pope, *The Rape of the Lock*

Anne's uncle, King Charles II, expressed his opinion of Anne's husband, Prince George of Denmark: "I have tried him drunk and I have tried him sober and there is nothing in him."

Queen Anne 1702 - 1714

After J. Closterman, National Portrait Gallery, London

Brown hair, blue eyes; dress, gold silk brocade; girdle around waist: gilt metal with pearls. Garter collar, dark blue circled garters with gold edging and mottos, red centers with gilt design and gilt bows between garters. St. George and the dragon, which hangs in the center, is white, red and gilt. Robe: crimson velvet with ermine lining.

Take what you can get, was the old monarch's maxim. He was not a lofty monarch, certainly; he was not a patron of the fine arts; but he was not a hypocrite, he was not revengeful, he was not extravagant. Though a despot in Hanover, he was a moderate ruler in England. His aim was to leave it to itself as much as possible, and to live out of it as much as he could. His heart was in Hanover.

—William Makepeace Thackeray,
The Four Georges

Brown hair, blue eyes; white cravat; armor: blackened metal. Crimson velvet robe edged with white ermine. Royal Blue sash over shoulder. White shoes with silver buckle. White breeches and hose; gold sword belt, gilt sword hilt, white metal blade.

George I
1714 - 1727

After J. Vanderbank,
Royal Collection

The Sun, we saw precede,
Those mighty Joys restor'd,
Gave to our future Need,
From great PLANTAGENET a Lord.
From whose high Veins this greater Day arose,
A Second GEORGE, to fix our World's
Repose,
From CHARLES restor'd, short was our Term
of Bliss,
But GEORGE from GEORGE entails our
Happiness.

—Colley Cibber, The Poet Laureate;
from his Birthday Ode, 1731

Around the royal table spread,
See how the beauteous branches shine!
Sprung from the fertile genial bed
Of glorious GEORGE and CAROLINE.
While Heav'n with bounteous hand
Has so enrich'd our store;
When shall this promis'd land
In royal heirs be poor?
All we can further ask, or Heav'n bestow,
Is, that we long this happiness may know.

—Colley Cibber,
from his Brithday Ode, 1732

George's children weren't even good-looking. No wonder Samuel Johnson, after describing how great poets such as Virgil had written immortal praise of great monarchs such as Augustus, unkindly wrote:

Great George's acts let tuneful Cibber sing;
For Nature form'd the Poet for the King.

And no wonder George II said, with his thick German accent, "I hate all Boets and Bainters."

White hair, black queue; black hat, black cockade, gold lace, gilt button. Scarlet coat, gold lace, gilt buttons. White shirt and neckcloth. Silver Garter star on breast, with blue Garter and red cross. Scarlet breeches; black boots. Gilt sword, black scabbard with brass tip. Gold and crimson sword knot. Gold and crimson sword belt. Royal Blue sash across chest.

George II 1727 - 1760

After Wootton, 1742, National Army Museum

White hair, blue eyes; scarlet coat, dark blue cuffs and collar; gold lace, gilt buttons. Garter star on breast: silver, with blue garter and red cross. White shirt and neckcloth; white breeches and waistcoat; gilt buttons. Royal Blue sash across chest; garter on leg: dark blue and gold. Black shoes, gilt buckle. Black hat with gold lace black cockade, gold button and cord. Gold watch fob. Gilt sword, black scabbard, gilt fittings. Sword knot: gold and crimson.

George III
1760 - 1820
After Zoffany, Royal Collection

As monarchs possessed less actual power, their official poets gave them ever-higher praise.

Had these blest Bards been call'd, to pay
The vows of this auspicious day,
Each had confess'd a fairer throne,
A mightier sovereign than his own!
Chaucer had made his hero-monarch yield
The martial fame of Cressy's well-fought field
To peaceful prowess, and the conquests calm,
That braid the sceptre with the patriot's palm;
His chaplets of fantastic bloom,
His colorings, warm from Fiction's loom,
Spenser had cast in scorn away,
And deck'd with truth alone the lay;
All real here, the Bard had seen
The glories of his pictur'd Queen!
The tuneful Dryden had not flatter'd here,
His lyre had blameless been, his tribute
all sincere!
—Thomas Warton, "Birthday Ode, 1787"

All this was too much for the comic poet Peter Pindar:

But, Thomas Warton, without joking,
Art thou, or art thou not, thy Sovereign
smoking? [pulling his leg]
How canst thou seriously declare
That George the Third
With Cressy's Edward can compare,
Or Harry?—'Tis too bad, upon my word:
George is a clever King, I needs must own,
And cuts a jolly figure on the Throne.
—Peter Pindar,
"Instructions to a Celebrated Laureate"

In her *Diary*, Fanny Burney recorded an encounter with the King:

"Was there ever," cried he, "such stuff as great part of Shakespeare? Only one must not say so! But what think you? —what? —Is there not sad stuff?—what?—what?"

"Yes, indeed, I think so, sir, though mixed with such excellences, that—"

"Oh," cried he, laughing good humoredly, "I know it is not to be said! but it's true. Only it's Shakespeare, and nobody dare abuse him."

When George first met Princess Caroline of Brunswick, a few days before he was scheduled to marry her, her appearance and manners distressed him. His first remark was, "Harris, I am not well; pray get me a glass of brandy."

When he left, Caroline expressed the opinion that George was not as good-looking as his portraits. The marriage went from bad to worse, and it is recorded that when George came into a room where his friends were discussing Wellington's great victories over the French in the west of Spain, George's comment was, "D—n the west! D—n the east! D—n Wellington! The question is, *How* am I to rid myself of this d—ned Princess of Wales?" His later divorce action against the Queen was sensational and scandalous, and brought the monarchy into disrepute, but the House of Lords voted against the divorce. How far the monarchy had fallen in power since the days of Henry VIII: George IV couldn't even get one divorce!

.... He leads a most extraordinary life —never gets up till six in the afternoon. They come to him and open the window curtains at six or seven o'clock in the morning; he breakfasts in bed, does whatever business he can be brought to transact in bed too, he reads every newspaper quite through, dozes three or four hours, gets up in time for dinner, and goes to bed between ten and eleven. He sleeps very ill, and rings his bell forty times in the night; if he wants to know the hour, though a watch hangs close to him, he will have his valet de chambre down rather than turn his head to look at it. The same thing if he wants a glass of water; he won't stretch out his hand to get it. His valets are nearly destroyed.

—Charles Greville, *Memoirs*

George IV 1820 - 1830

After Lawrence, National Portrait Gallery

Brown hair, blue eyes; black stock around neck; scarlet coatee with dark blue collar and cuffs; gold lace and embroidery on collar and cuffs; gilt buttons. Gold aiguilette. Orders around neck: red ribbon, gold order with red and black. Royal Blue sash across shoulder; crimson sash around waist; waist belt: gold with two small crimson stripes, gold clasp. White breeches, black boots; black hat, white plume. Gold bullion tassel. Buff gloves, gilt spurs. Order stars on chest: silver.

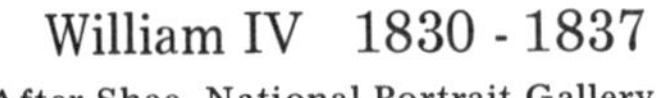

William IV 1830 - 1837

After Shee, National Portrait Gallery

The present King and his proceedings occupy all attention, and nobody thinks any more of the late King than if he had been dead fifty years, unless it be to abuse him and to rake up all his vices and misdeeds. Never was elevation like that of King William IV. His life has been hitherto passed in obscurity and neglect, in miserable poverty, surrounded by a numerous progeny of bastards. . . . There never was anything like the enthusiasm with which he was greeted by all ranks; though he has trotted about both town and country for sixty-four years, and nobody ever turned round to look at him, he cannot stir now without a mob, patrician as well as plebeian, at his heels. . . . The King's good-nature, simplicity, and affability to all about him are very striking, and in his elevation he does not forget any of his old friends and companions. He was in no hurry to take upon himself the dignity of King nor to throw off the habits and manners of a country gentleman. Altogether he seems a kind-hearted, well-meaning, not stupid, burlesque, bustling old fellow, and if he doesn't go mad may make a very decent King, but he exhibits oddities. All odd, and people are frightened, but his wits will at least last till the new Parliament meets. . . .

The other night the King had a party, and at eleven o'clock he dismissed them thus: "Now, ladies and gentlemen, I wish you a good night. I will not detain you any longer from your amusements, and shall go to my own, which is to go to bed; so come along, my Queen."

—from Charles Greville, *Memoirs*

White hair, blue eyes; white stock and shirt ruffle; white waistcoat and breeches, white stockings; Blue coat; lace on collar, cuffs and lapels, gold. Gilt buttons. Order star on chest: silver. Royal Blue sash; gold watch fob. White coat lining. Black shoes with silver buckles. Black hat with gold lace edging. Black cockade, gilt button. Gilt sword; gold sword knot, black scabbard with gilt fittings.

. . . But she—but she
Was loved as monarch ne'er was loved before
From girlhood unto womanhood, and grew,
Fresh as the leaf, and fragrant as the flower,
In grace and comeliness until the day
Of happy nuptial, glad maternity,
More closely wedded to her people's heart,
By each fresh tie that knitted her to him,
Whose one sole thought was how she still might be
Helpmate to England . . .
—Alfred Austin, from "Victoria the Wise"

The great tragedy of Victoria's life was her loss of her husband, Prince Albert, in 1861. Her subjects sympathized with her grief.

Break not, O woman's heart, but still endure:
Break not, for thou art Royal, but endure,
Remembering the beauty of that star
Which shone so close beside Thee that ye made
One light together, but has past and leaves
The Crown a lonely splendor.
—Alfred Tennyson, from "Dedication" of *Idylls of the King*

England flourished under Victoria's reign.

Long may each zone its wealth profusely pour
Upon her laplike, peace-protected shore!
Long may the strain come swelling from
the ships,
Which keeps Victoria on a nation's lips!
Long, long in thousand eyes that smile be seen
Which thinks her woman, though it hails
her Queen:
Queen, wife, or mother, perfect in each part,
And throned securely in a People's heart!
—Alfred Austin, from *The Season*

Dark brown hair, blue eyes; crown: gold, silver heavily laden with diamonds and various precious gems.Gold pall, or mantel; gold waistcords, gold sceptre. White undergarment.

Queen Victoria 1837 - 1901
After Hayter, Royal Collection

Edward VII 1901 - 1910

when Prince of Wales as Colonel-in-Chief, Gordon Highlanders

In 1905 King Edward was asked to restore diplomatic relations with Serbia, but refused to do so until the last of the assassins of the previous king had been banished from the new king's court. "And besides this reason, I have another, and so to say, a personal reason. *Mon métier à moi est d'être Roi.* [My trade is to be king.] King Alexander was also by his métier 'un Roi.' As you see, we belonged to the same guild, as laborers or professional men. I cannot be indifferent to the assassination of a member of my profession, or, if you like, a member of my guild. We should be obliged to shut up our businesses if we, the Kings, were to consider the assassinations of kings as of no consequence at all. I regret, but you see that I cannot do what you wish me to do."

—Edward Legge,
King Edward in his True Colors

"You can tell when you have crossed the frontier into Germany because of the badness of the coffee."

—King Edward VII

With King Edward's passing we lost a lovable, wayward and human monarch. He was one who came to decisions by instinct and not by logic, and rarely made a mistake in his judgment of men. On the whole, he preferred the society of the female sex and was never happier than in the company of pretty women. . . . The King's great attraction was that he was a very good listener. During the interviews and audiences, no matter on what subject, he was always able to fix his attention on his visitor. . . . The pleasure of giving never seemed to diminish with King Edward. Most very rich men are so imposed upon and meet with so little gratitude that they derive no pleasure after a time from being generous, and develop into stingy men, but King Edward up to the end took great pleasure in giving presents or in doing someone a kind action. He was by nature the most generous of men, and it was this trait in his character that induced him to give so many decorations. He liked the obvious pleasure it gave the recipient. At any game of cards he disliked losing intensely, but loved paying his losses and did so as if he were making his opponent a present.

—Sir Frederick Ponsonby,
Recollections of Three Reigns

EDWARD VII (left)

Grey-brown beard, blue eyes. Glengarry: dark blue with red, white and green dicing. Black cockade. Silver badge. Doublet: scarlet with yellow collar and cuffs. Gold lace on collar and cuffs and on skirt flaps. Gilt buttons. Silver order stars. Medals, various colors. Gold aiguilette; plaid brooch: silver. Belted plaid and trews: wide dark green stripe on dark blue background. Yellow stripe through middle of the dark green stripe. Sword and scabbard: silver. Sword knot, gold. Waistbelt: gold. Beltplate, gilt with silver badge. Black shoes.

George V 1910 - 1936

"Wake up, England!"
—speech in 1901, while Prince of Wales

from a letter of instructions to his son, the future George VI, who was returning from a tour of Australia and New Zealand: "We will not embrace at the station before so many people. When you kiss Mama take yr. hat off."

"If I may be regarded as in some true sense the head of this great and wide-spread family, sharing its life and sustained by its affection, this will be a full reward for the long and sometimes anxious labors of my reign."
—George V's Christmas broadcast, 1934

commenting on the demonstrations of loyalty at his Jubilee in 1935: "I'd no idea they felt like that about me. I am beginning to think they must like me for myself."

"How is the empire?"
—last words

GEORGE V (right)

Blue eyes, grey brown hair; dark blue tunic with red collar and cuffs; gold embroidery on collar and cuffs, gold shoulder cords; yellow metal buttons. Pouch belt: gold with red cording center; Royal Blue sash; gold aigulettes. Order stars on chest, white, cross in center of top star, red; waistbelt, gold with red stripe in center. Helmet, silver, edging and chin strap, brass, spike and ball on top, gilt. Wreath and garter collar around star, gilt. Garter star, silver with blue garter in center. Red cross within blue garter. Red plume. White breeches, black boots; sword, white metal with brass mountings; sword knot, gold and crimson. White gloves; medals: crosses white, the rest, light yellow. Ribbons of various colors.

King George V as Colonel-in-Chief of the Royal Horse Guards

Edward VIII 1936

"I have found it impossible to carry the heavy burden of responsibility and to discharge my duties as King as I would wish to do without the help and support of the woman I love."
—radio speech upon abdicating

Blue eyes; lungi (turban) dark blue with gold and white bars; kurta (tunic), khaki; shoulder chains: white metal; collar badges, silver; buttons, yellow metal. Pouch belt: gold with red stripe in center; whistle and chain, silver. Medals, yellow metal, ribbons of various colors. Kummerbund, red with blue and gold Kashmir pattern. Breeches, khaki, boots, brown; sword, white metal, sword knot, gold and crimson, waistbelt, gold with central red stripe.

King Edward VIII when Prince of Wales, Commander-in-Chief, 35/36th Jacobs Horse, 1921

"Take care of the children and the country will take care of itself."

—George VI

from the King's diary September 3rd, 1939—the day World War II began: "At the outbreak of war at midnight of August 4th-5th 1914, I was a midshipman, keeping the middle watch on the bridge of H.M.S. 'Collingwood' at sea, somewhere in the North Sea. I was 18 years of age.

"In the Grand Fleet everyone was pleased that it had come at last. We had been trained in the belief that War between Germany and this country had to come one day, and when it did come we thought we were prepared for it. We were not prepared for what we found a modern war really was, and those of us who had been through the Great War never wanted another.

"Today we are at War again, and I am no longer a midshipman in the Royal Navy.

"In this grave hour, perhaps the most fateful in our history, I send to every household of my peoples, both at home and overseas, this message, spoken with the same depth of feeling for each one of you as if I were able to cross your threshold and speak to you myself.

"For the second time in the lives of most of us we are at war. Over and over again we have tried to find a peaceful way out of the differences between ourselves and those who are now our enemies. But it has been in vain. We have been forced into a conflict. For we are called, with our allies, to meet the challenge of a principle which, if it were to prevail, would be fatal to any civilized order in the world.

"It is the principle which permits a state, in the selfish pursuit of power, to disregard its treaties and its solemn pledges; which sanctions the use of force, or threat of force, against the sovereignty and independence of other states. Such a principle, stripped of all disguise, is surely the mere primitive doctrine that Might is Right. And if this principle were established throughout the world, the freedom of our own country and of the whole British Commonwealth of Nations would be in danger. But far more than this—the peoples of the world would be kept in the bondage of fear, and all hopes of settled peace and of the security of justice and liberty among nations would be ended.

"This is the ultimate issue which confronts us. For the sake of all that we ourselves hold dear, and of the world's order and peace, it is unthinkable that we should refuse to meet the challenge.

"It is to this high purpose that I now call my people at home and my peoples across the Seas, who will make our cause their own. I ask them to stand calm and firm and united in this time of trial. The task will be hard. There may be dark days ahead, and war can no longer be confined to the battlefield. But we can only do the right as we see the right, and reverently commit our cause to God. If one and all we keep resolutely faithful to it, ready for whatever service or sacrifice it may demand, then, with God's help, we shall prevail. May He bless and keep us all."

—The King's war broadcast

Brown hair, blue eyes; tunich and trousers Air Force blue; gold on collar, cuffs, epaulettes, buttons, aigulettes; white gloves and cross on chest; Garter star has blue circle with red cross; cap, black with gold cord and badge; sword brass hilt and fittings, black scabbard, gold knot. Waistbelt: central stripe of Air Force blue, outer stripes gold, gold belt plate. Black shoes.

George VI 1936 - 1952
as Marshal of the Royal Air Force

"My whole life, whether it be long or short, shall be devoted to your service and the service of our great imperial family to which we all belong, but I shall not have strength to carry out this resolution alone unless you join in it with me."

—radio speech on her twenty-first birthday (1947)

Hair, dark brown; eyes blue; cap, black. Cap badge: silver star with gold center; cockade: black; tunic, scarlet. Collar, cuffs and shoulder straps, dark blue. Gold embroidery on collar, cuffs and shoulder straps. White piping around collar and cuffs. Yellow buttons. Shoulder sash: Royal Blue. Aiguilettes, gold. Silver Garter Star. Blue Garter on star; red cross. Skirt and boots: black, white gloves. Waist sash: alternate red and crimson stripes, gold fringe. Saddle cloth: dark blue with gold lace and fringe. Brown horse and harness; brass rosettes and chain.

Elizabeth II 1952 -

H. M. Queen Elizabeth II in uniform of Colonel-in-Chief, Scots Guards